# *Love in the Time of Covid*

# Love in the Time of Covid

Poems of Spiritual Introspection

## Anna Cates

ESOURCE *Publications* • Eugene, (

LOVE IN THE TIME OF COVID
Poems of Spiritual Introspection

Resource Publications
An Imprint of Wipf and Stock Publishers
199 W. 8th Ave., Suite 3
Eugene, OR 97401

www.wipfandstock.com

PAPERBACK ISBN: 978-1-6667-0366-5
HARDCOVER ISBN: 978-1-6667-0370-2
EBOOK ISBN: 978-1-6667-0371-9

JULY 20, 2021

For all the sweet kitties in my life

Love never fails.

*1 CORINTHIANS 13:8*

# Contents

*Love in the Time of Covid*

*Tanka, Kyōka, & Haiga*

*Haiku & Senryu*

# Acknowledgments

Haibun, tanka prose, and sequences in this collection previously appeared in:

*Abyss & Apex*: "Zen"
*Ephemerae*: "Shintai"
*Mock Turtle*: "Night Song," "[Scratch & Sniff Ku]"
*Femku*: "American Pie," "The Cure," "Long Drive Home"
*Failed Haiku: A Journal of English Senryu*: "Heartland, USA (sic)," "Stranger," "Casanova," "Small Gatherings," "Circus," "2021 New Year's Resolution"
*Otoliths*: "Old Faithful," "July 2020," "Antiquarian," "E. M."
*Open: Journal of Arts & Letters*: "After Gloaming," "2020," "Love in the Time of Covid"
*Drifting Sands*: "The Enchantment," "Revelation"
*The Other Bunny*: "Recipes," "The Penalty"
*Contemporary Haibun Online*: "One Out of Four," "Antique Dealer," "Summer Move," "The Poison Tree"
*Scifaikuest*: "After Atlantis"
*Bamboo Hunt*: "Catku"

Tanka and kyōka in this collection, some with minor edits, previously appeared in:

*Failed Haiku: A Journal of English Senryu*: "chocolate," "dirty bottles"
*Tinywords*: "dappled blue,"
*Skylark*: "a marsh wren"

*Eucalypt*: "black holes," "he didn't believe," "Spring 2020"

*Otata*: "monarch," "skeletal moon"

*Noon*: "in her breath"

*Presence*: "golden leaves," "crying for food," "cricket song"

*Kokako*: "spring outing," Nazi ruins"

*Under the Basho*: "worn cobblestones"

*Ribbons*: "summer moon," "sunrise," "dip and splash," "how sweet the shade"

*One Man's Maple Moon*: "a dead skunk's"

*Undertow Tanka Review*: "after spring rain," "dark sky"

*Bamboo Hut*: "white pines," "the old oak," "cloudy sky," "blue bird," "weaving through," "conch shell," "a silent puppet," "musty Victorian," "a brown thrasher," "veiled stars," "a barred owl," "hollow moon," "first raindrops"

*Cattails*: "purple smokes," "shrunken creek," "a mothball rolls," "why is it," "passing days," "October frost," "country roads"

*Atlas Poetica*: "Silent Spring"

*Tanka Journal*: "gourmet pizza," "autumn moon," "luminous snowfall," "a fallen apple"

*Never Ending Story*: "Theory of Relativity," "fireflies"

*Frameless Sky*: "windstorm," "an eagle," "close of day,""a cherry tree"

*Undertow Tanka Review*: "I peer," "dead fawn," "cemetery breeze," "cold night," "grill smoke," "dusky sky," "morning frost," "setting sun," "cold earth"

*25 Tanka about Arthropds*: "inching forward"

Haiku and senryu in this collection, some with minor edits, previously appeared in:

*Modern Haiku, Frogpond, Haiku Canada, Bones, Femku, Scifaikuest, Poetry Quarterly, World Haiku Review, Cattails, Bottle Rockets, Ginyu, Wild Plum, 50 Haikus, Haiku Journal, Three Line Poetry, Failed Haiku, Wild Plum, Under the Basho, Blueline, Stardust Haiku, Bamboo Hut, Presence, Taj Mahal Review, Ardea, Inner Voices, Caribbean Kigo Kukai, European*

# ACKNOWLEDGMENTS

*Quarterly Kukai, 7X20, Akitsu Quarterly, Wales Haiku Journal, Autumn Moon, Kokako, Ink Sweat and Tear, Haiku Dialogue.*

Ohio Poetry Day award-winners:

"gentle breezes stir . . ." Third Place winner in Ohio Poetry Day Association's 2016 *Haiku for Betty Contest* and published in *Ohio Poetry Day Best of 2016* anthology.
"Christmas lights . . ." First Place winner *Caribbean Kigo Kukai* 106 (Dec. 15, 2015).

# Introduction

*Love in the Time of Covid* is the sequel to *The Journey*, my earlier collection of mixed form poems on the theme of religion. *Love in the Time of Covid* continues that poetic journey with short form poems that reveal the intersection of nature and spirituality. Finally, it highlights my unlikely friendship with an antiquarian of rare oddities during the Covid-19 crisis and beyond.

    *Love in the Time of Covid* is a collection of traditional Japanese short form poems: haiku, senryu, tanka, kyōka, haibun, tanka prose, and haiku sequences. Thus, a few words about short form poetry might be clarifying.

    *Haiku* detail reality in fragmented sequences of "aha moments," in keenly perceived segments of place and time. Rich with natural imagery, haiku reveal the relationship between the human condition and nature. As human beings are both spiritual and natural beings, living in harmony with nature, under God, becomes a means to peace and contentment. Haiku's sensitivity to nature becomes an avenue to witness "natural revelation," prompting recognition of God.

    As haiku enthusiasts know, composing "modern" haiku is not about counting syllables. However, brevity is essential to the form, making seventeen syllables total a tentative maximum per poem. Yet some haikuists like to see line two longer than lines one and three, to harken back to the 5/7/5 syllabic pattern that many associate with the form. But there is flexibility, even experimentality, with short form poetry. Successful haiku, like poetry in general, involves the right words in the right order, freshness of language and originality. Modern haiku can feature one line, two lines, or three lines or more, but lines are very short, sometimes a single syllable! All other Japanese short forms draw from the haiku.

*Senryu* (pronounced "send you") is structurally identical to haiku yet differs in subject matter and tone. Senryu are more satiric or humorous, often hinting at human folly.

*Tanka* might be understood as haiku followed by two additional lines of about seven syllables a piece, maximum. The extra lines offer insight into the images within the first three lines. Tanka often feature a melancholy tone of reflection.

*Kyōka* are structurally identical to tanka yet differ in subject matter and tone. Kyōka are a more parodic form.

*Haibun* combine one or more haiku or senryu with prose. The title, haiku, and prose sections of a haibun are meant to harmonize with each other but not repeat each other's diction.

*Tanka prose* combines tanka, or kyōka, with prose in a manner similar to haibun.

A *haiku sequence* is a series of three or more interrelated haiku, with each haiku serving as a stanza. A haiku sequence might seem like just a small poem, or a poem of short line stanzas, to readers unfamiliar with traditional Japanese short forms.

Two additional forms are *renga*, collaborative poetry involving multiple poets, and *haiga*, art or photography combined with haiku or tanka, alternatively termed "tankart." There is much to appreciate in these dynamic poetic forms.

# *One*

## [Scratch & Sniff Ku]

# [SCRATCH & SNIFF KU]

green fields
glisten with dew
[strawberry]

a feral dog
tracks through the mist
[wildflowers]

a grackle
sings on a broken branch
[pine needles]

crickets
serenade the starlight
[fresh rain]

# NIGHT SONG

a horned owl
glides to the moon
rippling starlight

mercurial eyes
peer through the gloom
the darkness bright

the owl
returns through a wormhole
long trek to sunlight

song of clouds
drifting over the magic moon
the owl rides it

naked branches
the owl lands
in the calligraphy

# AFTER ATLANTIS

a skiff rocks
in ghost-stirred mists . . .
icy barnacles

clouds
close over the moon—
albatross song

a lemming
leaps off a cliff . . .
sound of water

## ZEN

glinting zodiac
a crooked pine points toward . . .

crescent moon
crusting lava flow & . . .

bamboo dripping
water over prayer stones . . .

between the worm
and bird-watching cat . . .

a Buddhist monk
alive on fire . . .

Zen

# SHINTAI[1]

I

cherry blooms
looming behind reflections
the pagoda

II

scarlet sky
the blood memories
of a katana

III

pearl hairclip
the geisha's grin
matching

1. Objects worshipped near Shinto shrines

## E. M.

he was man
of clever disguise—
a burlap bag

he braved the spotlight
and the crowds—
a solitary star

he made teen girls
scream—
his trunk hung low

he lived fast
and died fast—
the Elephant Man

# THE ENCHANTMENT

Mughal Age[1] Maratha[2] poets maintained all could acquire the Highest regardless of caste. Bhakti[3] alone provided redemption. They posed in song the erotic metaphor under the eminent Emperor Akbar and the elephants danced![4]

sitar strains
pooling in a lotus bloom
wet shadows

1. A Muslim dynasty, Turkic-Mongol in origin, that reigned in northern India from the 16th to mid-18th centuries

2. An Indian caste

3. Worship of one supreme deity

4. Parrinder, *World Religions*, 192–240.

# DESCENDANT

Pagans of old reveled beside the yggdrasil, the sacred tree, uniting nine worlds. Beneath a drunken moon, moist and shimmering post-coitus, creation mythology burbled up from the void. Fire and ice gods, giants, and the trickster, Loki, mingled with Nerthu, benevolent Mother Earth. The villagers washed her emblem in the lake before the slaves' sacrificial drowning. Inside the tomb the dead lived on, obliging grave-goods for ghostly feasts. Mars gleamed above bubbling cauldrons. Leaders bull-baited and blood-sacrificed. Big-breasted goddesses and gods in antlers brawled in blood feuds, amassing skulls. Bull-horned, wild, and war-mongering phallic gods arose to haunt battlefields. Bird-like hags and all varieties of the mystical macabre arbitrated magical rites. Queen Morrigan of phantoms dangled her amassed head trophies. Valhalla valkyries and blood-christening witches rode wargs and wove guts into looms. Yesterday's gloom, these deified ultracrepidarians. Within rising mists strange gods linger . . .[1]

the fresh scent
of 10,000 weeds . . .
prayer trail

---

1. Parrinder, *World Religions*, 101–113.

## AFTER GLOAMING

Like many children, she was afraid of the dark, when the world outside her bedroom window disappeared when the lights turned on at night, which only made the darkness darker.

She imagined the world outside the window shifting into a parallel reality. There roamed wolves and bears, ready to devour her.

She confessed her suspicion about the wolves and bears to her mother, but Mother only laughed, saying there was no such danger, no wolves and bears, lurking in the dark.

antique quilt . . .
our hodgepodge
of sunsets

# SUMMER MOVE

dust resettles
on a country road . . .
empty sky
always in such a hurry
to end up nowhere


July 2006. I pull into the gravel driveway of my parents' next
rental, an old farmhouse, surrounded by cornfields and a row of
lonely white pines.

I stand on the lawn with Dad, elderly now, and forced to wear
Depends. But due to financial constraints, he still works, as a tutor
for a rich man's foster sons.

The old farmhouse plumbing is sluggish, and they're worried
about rodents. Striving for optimism, I gesture toward the fields.
"You've got all the free corn you can eat here!"

Dad, who also farmed for many years, peers at the rustling
tassels and shakes his head.

"Why not?" I ask, assuming he's opposed to stealing on moral
grounds.

"It's not fit for human consumption."

I'm surprised, and almost amused. He's not opposed to a few
free ears of corn, just worried about the quality. "What's wrong
with it?"

"It's not 'sweet corn.' It's gmo, grown for cattle feed. Too many
pesticides."

My smile fades, as the ire flickers within me. I flail my arms. I
can only wonder about the well water.

a coon peers
from a hollow tree . . .
ragged clouds
one day following another
just scraping by

# RECIPES

red bird
frantic at the pane . . .
pandemic


ANTI-VIRAL DANDELION SOUP:
—Dandelion greens, thoroughly washed
—1–2 cloves fresh garlic
—1 tablespoon finely diced fresh ginger
—Soup base, stock, or bullion (to taste)
Instructions: Bring to a boil; then turn down heat and simmer for about 15 minutes. Note: Don't spray your lawns to remove dandelions. Dandelions are medicine! We dump enough toxic substances into the environment. Give your lawns, bees, and stray cats a break!


ANTI-VIRAL NO BAKE COOKIES:
—1 cup *raw** honey (anti-viral)
—½ cup coconut oil (anti-viral)
—½ cup cocoa powder (antioxidants)
—1 cup nut butter of choice (nut butter + oats = a complete protein)
—3 cups quick oats (nut butter + oats = a complete protein)
—1 teaspoon vanilla extract
Instructions: Mix wet ingredients. Mix in oats. Spoon into cookie shapes and chill until hardened. *Raw* honey has medicinal properties heated honey may lack. Note: Don't feed babies under 1-year of age honey. Their digestive systems are underdeveloped, and it may kill them!

forsythia buds . . .
how quiet the town
after shutdown

## 2020

After shutdown, I watched them the whole lonely afternoon, alone on the beach, mother and daughter. The geese have yet to return.

the red balloon
escapes over the briny waves—
March gales
so briefly they are ours
before slipping from our grasp

# STRANGER

Recently, someone completely unknown to me contacted me via Facebook. She hoped I could help her form a liaison between an elderly man she's a caregiver for and his biological sons, relatives of mine, raised by another man. "He's over 80, in a wheelchair," she said. "He wants to see them."

I called his oldest son on the phone, but he expressed reluctance in connecting with his biological father. ". . . not after all this time," he said.

I felt a little sorry for the elderly man. Father's Day was rapidly approaching. I could picture him, withered and hunched over in his wheelchair, reassessing his life, wanting closure, regretting that, due to mistakes he'd made, he'd lost the chance to raise the sons he'd fathered. He wanted to be a real Dad. He wanted to be like that cloud that's really a god, who exhales, forming the wind . . .

animal crackers,
animal clouds . . .
childhood

## THE CURE

As a follow up to the mammogram, at my doctor's urging, I set a
date for an ultrasound . . .

*Maybe if I inject something, a disinfectant, some kind of household
cleaner, maybe that would dissolve any nodules . . .*

white noise . . .
pressing the off button
daily accomplishment

# REVELATION

A pastor returned to a church he'd previously ministered at after an absence of several years. He seemed older, huskier, and somehow, more Irish-looking. Something was decidedly different about his nose, smaller, a pug nose. *Rhinoplasty*, I mused. *A botched nose job*! I marveled at such an example of private insecurities. Why would a middle-aged man, needing to focus on spiritual things, have been so concerned about something so petty? His nose had never been unsightly or unusual, neither in shape nor size. He'd moved to the deep south to preach at another church. *Did he offend someone and get beat-up, necessitating reconstructive surgery? Was his congregation African American; maybe he was he trying to be like Michael Jackson, turning somersaults, jumping through rings of fire to reach his flock* . . .

Weeks later, it finally occurred to me what might have happened: skin cancer surgery. Like the ears that stick out from a John Deere hat, the nose can be a problem area for sun exposure.

the skinny legs
of a praying mantis . . .
heat spell

# JULY 2020

red sky/red eyes/red lines on graphs—

Desperate times . . . Death tolls rising . . . Adding to the chaos, someone hacks my personal email account. Using my email address, the hacker spams pleas for money to dozens of my contacts, including members of the haiku community . . .

Bob Lucky[2]
stranded in Saudi Arabia
covid senryu

2. A haikuist and editor

# CIRCUS

big top—
wa!king the wire
in c!own feet

an oversized mouth
choking on shoe !aces—
yak woman

sticking his neck out
po!itica!!y—
giraffe vs. !ion tamer . . .

High up in the stands, stashed in shadow, unnoticed by the crowds,
the arch fiend, Satan, hunches on the bleacher, still as thin ice.
Hints of brimstone halo him, his snakeskin boots freshly oiled and
glistening, his anal rash on fire . . .

popcorn spills—
the train rolls on
into quiet places

## ONE OUT OF FOUR[1]

I'm in the kitchen, chopping organic beets. I feel a familiar sensation running down my thighs. I hasten to the bathroom. I'm already wearing a tampon, but this spotting is nothing like my menstrual blood of yesteryear, watery and absorbable. It's like a tampon-resistant slime that moves around the tampon on its determined migration down into my pink slippers . . .

perimenopause?
ah . . . the many shades
of dark slacks

I sit across from my gynecologist, staring down into the face of his humming laptop. He looks up, and I smile, ready for him to tell me the good news, that I'm perfectly healthy and that my symptoms are just part of a normal stage of life. Yet he seems so sober.

"I'm sorry I don't have better news," he says.

"What do you mean?"

"Didn't you log into the portal and read your biopsy results?"

"No. I didn't realize I could do that."

"You have uterine cancer . . ." He goes on to tell me the various parts of my reproductive system that he can remove as part of a treatment process.

Reeling with denial, my head juts forward. "You are *not* removing any lymph nodes!"

---

1. The number of people who will get cancer at some point in their life

Upon my boyfriend's advice, I travel out of town for a second opinion. I seek, via email, input from a radiation oncologist in my writers' group. Eventually, I resign myself to reality.

cold November
the melancholy cry
of a night bird

# HEARTLAND, USA (SIC)

I

a Choctaw elder
recalls Woodstock . . .
wilted cosmos

II

pilgrimage . . .
beyond old brick buildings
meat processing plant

III

sirens . . .
a paranoid poodle presses
its nose to the glass

IV

city cemetery . . .
in the slow-falling snow
a shadow lingers

## 2021 NEW YEAR'S RESOLUTION

The nations raged, but your wrath has come, and the time for
judging the dead . . . and for destroying those who destroy the earth.
—REV 11:18 NRSV


I decide to use less plastic.  I discover online Himalayan Jasmine
brown rice in a burlap bag for $12.99.  A burlap bag?  My mind
reels.  I hastily order four pounds.

The rice arrives covered in plastic bubble wrap.

fast food scents . . .
Waldo still lost
among the beasties

# OLD FAITHFUL

in Wyoming wilderness
a friend and I
paused in sight
of a steaming

geyser
while the sunset screamed
in orange and violet
*fire*!

      snow
      glistening in a dog bowl
      first stars

# CATKU

windy streets
an orange stray
missing fur tufts

bird calls
a cat's gifted vole
on the asphalt

big dogs and fast cars?
the world is wild
stay with me

spring friendship
the warmth
of a paw pad

little hon
a sexy catwalk
and a fluffy bum

# Two

Love in the Time of Covid

# NEIGHBORS

June 2019. With a little help from a dating site, I make a new friend.
He ends up being a little eccentric . . .

cold Valentine's Day
he reveals his stash
of funeral home teeth

"I bought it on eBay," he explains.
"Isn't that a bit macabre?" I ask.
He just laughs.

# AMERICAN PIE: A VIGNETTE

*for Tom*

first date . . .
the car he drives:
a funeral hearse!

beautiful day . . .
he sets up our candlelight
cemetery picnic

wet June . . .
I bake bran muffins
for a second date

country Victorian . . .
I calmly survey his
funeral home décor

July fireworks . . .
I bring the ice cream:
death by chocolate

his big bog
laden with peepers . . .
testing the waters

## LOVE IN THE TIME OF COVID

Spring 2020. No effervescent sparkles beside the fireplace. No wine glasses clinking. No strains from a violin. Only our "great adaptation," this social distancing . . .

pandemic longing for the daffodils to open

# SMALL GATHERINGS

Summer 2020. Life is not without its risks. Why not "break bread" with a friend?

I drive out to his Victorian farmhouse-turned-antiques-workshop and park behind his big white van . . .

Romanesque arches
beside the cupboard
Decameron dinner debate

I squint in disbelief at the expiration date on a jar of spaghetti sauce. "Twenty *thirteen*?" I ask. He just laughs . . .

old time charm
rock salt churning
orange sherbet sky

## ANTIQUE DEALER

I've grown used to his idiosyncrasies.  Still, he sometimes surprises
me.

an "average man"
with an "average life" . . .
used caskets

# ANTIQUARIAN

Halloween
full moon in four time zones
he calls me

touring
stockrooms of oddities—
his hazel eyes gleaming

one man's trash
another's treasure:
casket crucifix

vintage embalmer . . .
at his behest I read to him
a horror

alone in the quiet
the touch of his hand . . .
cold turkey

# CASANOVA

After distancing, he and I stage a get-together . . .

He puts me to work, dehulling black walnuts.

holiday pies . . .
waiting for the moonrise
Mars and Venus

# LONG DRIVE HOME

Returning from a doctor's appointment, a sign along the road detains my attention: *Foster parents needed . . .*

death toll
a hellish masquerade
stringing us along

## ADMISSIONS

lost child
digging through a tome
rainy Saturday

"I never wanted to have kids," he tells me.
"Most people do want them, eventually," I say.
"They ask too many questions—"
"All you have to do is answer them!"
I relay a quirky childhood tale: In the third grade, I had this crazy idea to amass a huge booger ball for the *Guinness Book of World Records* . . .
He remains unmoved.

hundreds of springs
the old oak dead now
thin mist

## THE POISON TREE

I stand at the crossroads and peer back at who I was. I nearly mistake it: a lifeless body slumped beneath the tree. I taste the bittersweet knot in my throat. *What have I done?* I draw closer, beholding, to my horror, only myself!

Poisoned apple—
Sunset's blazing venom
Through the branches . . .
Who would have guessed
The import of a snake?

*Three*

Tanka, Kyōka, & Haiga

# SPRING 2020

light snow
frosts a fallen bluebird
beneath the pear tree
the path ends in silence
silhouettes and shadows

yellow forsythia buds
struggling for joy
after shutdown
how quiet the town
tragic, this sacred silence

a silent puppet
in a chair by the window
musty Victorian
in forgotten rooms
yesterday's whispers


a mothball rolls
into attic silence
old hallmarks
from cold yesterdays
vanish in the dust

a dead skunk's
open mouth drinks
the cold rain
in a mushy field
I wait for honeysuckle


dead fawn
the yogurt meat
of vultures
picking over
the endless days

cloudy sky
a church cemetery
aging with oaks
in tall grass
mossy gravestones


cold earth
above our decay
fresh flowers
how time grinds rock
into dust

sunrise
dandelions & bees
this spring like another
I once loved . . .
before you went away


an eagle
shrinks with the climb
over the purple hills—
time will swallow
everything

conch shell
listening to wave rhythms
the flaming sunset
footprints swallowed by the tide
were we ever here?


hollow moon
hanging on till
tomorrow
it will come then go
before today ends

the old oak
is dead at last
the sound
of hollow wind
now it is gone


shrunken creek
spilling into dusk
ironweed
draws the last butterflies . . .
who too will soon be gone

fireflies
drift through the cemetery
summer's end
friends, strangers, enemies
fading into rest




cemetery breeze
spiriting fallen leaves
I cross the bike trail
stopping by fleeting shadows
remembering mulberries

cricket song
retreating into dusk
along the woodland trail
as the hollow moon fades
so will our sojourn


a brown thrasher
winters in the pine—
old strip mine
at the end of our labors
the silent darkness

windstorm . . .
a single shingle
lands in the grass
how everything crumbles
piece by piece


white pines
on some days
empty skies
shed no color
on the waters

Nazi ruins
a peaceful breeze
where inmates trod
the extra mile
lily of the valley


dark sky
wet stars raining
winter sleet—
stay beside the fire
outside it is cold, so cold

## SILENT SPRING

war-
no
more
war-
bling


blue bird
pecking grasses
for a nest
April's plea:
don't drop a bomb; plant a tree

inching forward
in his wheelchair
a one-legged vet
exploring the bike trail
yellow butterflies


gourmet pizza
at a sidewalk eatery
an atheist and a preacher
debate gay dads
fading sunlight

dirty bottles
tangled in honeysuckle
throwaway culture
politicians come and go
but plastic is permanent




chocolate
and a good romance
new divorcee
more compelling than truth
all our believable fictions

I peer
in streaming sunlight
and remember
80 percent of dust
is our own dead skin cells




grill smoke
after hot dogs
bread crusts for ducklings—
by the don't feed the birds sign
our anarchy

cold night
rain-washed pines glisten
in the moonlight
woods remember when once
were wolves howling


dusky sky
a disillusioned pink
beside dark waters
I lose belief
in the Lock Ness Monster

morning frost
wet toilet paper hangs
from the branches—
how the grins of chunked
jack-o-lanterns crumble


setting sun
a poet's pen
leaking
blood, sweat,
& daffodils

## THEORY OF RELATIVITY

                                    the eagle ascends
                          like an elusive truth
                  mountains
          fall farther
and farther away


summer moon
a cuckoo's midnight call
do not look
for me
I am gone

luminous snowfall
feeding the ocean's wail
as dusk deepens
we cannot turn back
standing at world's end


why is it
we only notice the hole
in the dinghy
once we reach
deep seas?

close of day
a blue beach towel
caught in the grass
the countless sands
the countless stars


golden leaves
on a Sunday drive
racing geese
to the sunset
to the moonrise

crying for food
beside the empty rental
an abandoned cat
what's left behind
life's empty bowl


a fallen apple
asleep in the grass
first stars
how quiet the twilight
at harvest's end

a barred owl
flirts with a birder
wet woods
in spring essence
concupiscence


spring outing
a child skips along
the serpent mound[1]
never completely catching
the archetypal egg

1. A prehistoric Native American effigy mound in the shape of a snake
swallowing an egg

a marsh wren
forages at the bank
autumn equinox
all streams flow back
to a mighty river


October frost
a blackbird loiters
on the asphalt . . .
how we strut with pride
pecking at crumbs

black holes
distances conjured in light years
within our universe
the child dazed by darkness
laden with stars and fears


in her breath,
a trace of onion . . .
mom tries to revise
my controversial
memories

a cherry tree
clings to its bloom . . .
within our steps
a little light
a little shadow, too




veiled stars
winding into oblivion
empty roads
how silent our secrets
how secret the silence

worn cobblestones—
pigeons wait for bread
at city center
she sits alone on the bench
while the last train whistles out


he didn't believe
her false tears, her lying tears
as the apple shed its bloom . . .
they were only tears, only tears
that he had made her cry

dip and splash
an orange bill fishes
by the lotus blooms
my lifetime spent searching
dusky depths for morsels




weaving through
a chain length fence
white thyme
the simple things
that surprise me

after spring rain
teetering on the branch
inchworm
I stand on the edge
verging on epiphany


purple smokes
clouds below clouds above
sprinkling rain
I almost glimpse the rainbow
before it vanishes

dappled blue
a Holstein heavy
in the morning haze
our leisurely pace
toward enlightenment


passing days
the soft hues of sunsets
spring through fall
they always come back to me
you always come back to me

skeletal moon
fireflies pass into
the porous dusk
we share its breath
ride the sacred river


monarch
& milkweed . . .
the last piece
of a puzzle
always fits

first raindrops
soak into parched loam
where woods wax wild
seeds sink so softly
into a thirsty soul


autumn moon
a stone path
through the woods
breaths of wind
I seek you

how sweet the shade
on the burbling brook
even from the bridge
to want is not to have
the gift of contentment

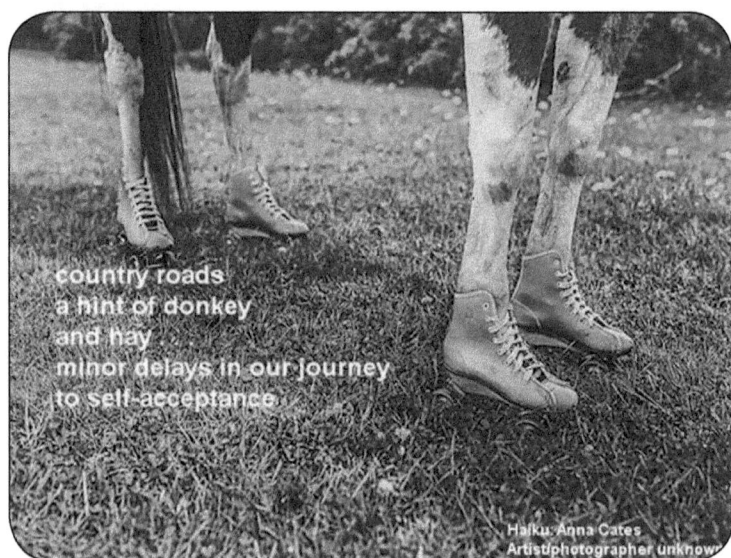

country roads
a hint of donkey
and hay
minor delays in our journey
to self-acceptance

Haiku: Anna Cates
Artist/photographer unknown

# The Penalty

You did not see because you did not look.
You weren't as bad as some, perhaps,
Yet priceless treasure you forsook.
You did not see because you did not look.
With Nazi friends, you burned the books,
You charred your heart, your chances lapsed.
You did not see because you did not look.
You weren't as bad as some? Perhaps . . .

      graveyard gargoyle—
      the doorman waits
      to receive you

# *Four*

## Haiku & Senryu

# MEDITATIONS ON PARADISE LOST

another
eve
holding
the red
delicious
naked
and alone

*Haiku Canada*

# CONSTRAINED POEM

[behindsilentwallsthenun'sclosedvagina]

*Femku*

new stars
a cold prayer stone
in my palm

*Scifaikuest*

desert places
where Jesus cursed
a fig tree

*Poetry Quarterly*

rain-washed dawn
veering toward oblivion
ant on a tea leaf

*World Haiku Review*

twilight
by the red-covered bridge
a frozen blackbird

*Cattails*




pepper patch
the cold bones
of a mole

*Bottle Rockets*




pine-scented fog
a cross in loose loam
only questions

*Ginyu*

attic sill
succumbing to dust
one dead moth

*Wild Plum*

ashen sky
I bypass
a black hearse

*50 haikus*

cold cemetery—
a flurry of whippoorwills
water-washed tombstones

*Haiku Journal*

barren limbs
above wet gravestones
a dirge of crows

*Three Line Poetry*

earth
still settling over the tomb
migrating birds

*Modern Haiku*

moving clouds . . .
the strange silence
of the gods

*Ginyu*

sunset
a buckeye bounces twice
before the tomb

*Modern Haiku*




Kroger . . .
a fellow shopper's "chin guard"
clearance cantaloupe

*Failed Haiku*




sea wall . . .
the loggerhead
that nearly made it

*Presence*

men in suits
with gospel tracts
mocking jay strains

*Failed Haiku*


October dusk
black oceans of doubt
in the 8 ball

*Wild Plum*


lone star
the church women ask
where I've been

*Failed Haiku*

October sunset
cold fog rises from the earth
among the tombstones

*Haiku Journal*


annual rings . . .
the many lives
you shaded

*Stardust Haiku*


tree of life?
the DNA I share
with lichen

*Failed Haiku*

cloud patterns lacking purpose pigweed

*Under the Basho*




wishing I knew
what birds know—
water poppy

*Blueline*




clear sky
the last cherry tomato
succumbs to frost

*Modern Haiku*

church bells
a child's toenails
Easter egg pink

*Modern Haiku*




spring breeze
cherry blossoms
holding on

*Taj Mahal Review*




still water
a gull's cry widens
the sky

*Modern Haiku*

fellowship meal devotees digest dogma

*Under the Basho*

church potluck
a hooker forks up
a wiener

*Under the Basho*

a gull glides
into dusk . . .
private regrets

*Stardust Haiku*

wet ashes
a preacher ponders
why churches burn

*Failed Haiku*


seminary . . .
a janitor dusting
corridors of light

*Bamboo Hut*


a jackal
heckles the sunset—
missiology

*Bones*

theatrical . . .
an angel's
broken halo

*Failed Haiku*

Mardi Gras
a demon rattling
green beads

*Presence*

white butterfly my good intentions . . .

*Failed Haiku*

nuclear talks—
John Kerry's false teeth
chattering

*Failed Haiku*

a dream
I want to remember
morning's chai tea

*Autumn Moon*

doorbell in April—
beyond lace curtains
Mormons with pamphlets

*Taj Mahal Review*

Easter dinner
I remember to bring
the potato salad

*Ardea*

sleepless night . . .
Richard Dawkins
on YouTube

*Failed Haiku*

day of rest
mowing the lawn
with sciatica

*Failed Haiku*

June wedding
missing at the altar
two cold feet

*Failed Haiku*

littered asphalt
a mother in hijab passes
the brothel

*Failed Haiku*

the statesman
and the beggar
distant stars

*Presence*

the wild apple
blooms apart from the hawthorn
our great divide

*Haiku Canada*




the icy wheels
of the bag lady's cart
rush hour

*Failed Haiku*




grebe tracks in the sand
he takes her hand . . .
soft tones of moonlight

*Kokako*

from acorn pith
a seedling flaunting
Kabbala

*Blueline*


whispers of God
a praying mantis glories
in lavender

*Ginyu*


the twisted neck
of a gifted squash
hican trees

*Stardust Haiku*

lady's mantle
the sunlight
on my shoulders

*Inner Voices*

gentle breezes stir
cherry blossom scent
halo of the moon

*Ohio Poetry Day*

convolvulus
crickets' Gregorian chant
amber sky

*European Quarterly Kukai*

Christmas mailing list
the old address book
obsolete now

*Bottle Rockets*

the UPS man
running behind
Yule moon

*Modern Haiku*

Christmas lights
I put the shadows
behind me

*First place winner, Caribbean Kigo Kukai*

Sunday morning bluebells ringing

*7X20*


lilac blooms
a lone Easter egg
in uncut grass

*Frogpond*


dusty Bible
an old bookmark stained
by a red pressed rose

*Three Line Poetry*

frosty moon
where inroads wind
bristlecone pine

*Kokako*

shady forests
swallowed whole by fire
one charred acorn

*Ink Sweat and Tears*

waning rose
an ant bears
my burden

*Ink Sweat and Tears*

Even in the desert
water drips from the mountain,
clouds roam.

*Ginyu*

a gypsy moth's
opening chrysalis . . .
endless skies

*European Quarterly Kukai*

peace moon
the milky taste
of saffron rice

*European Quarterly Kukai*

driftwood
smoothing over in time
our petty grievances

*Femku*




a great mountain
washed with rain—
I climb it

*Under the Basho*




a pilgrim pauses
along the trail
bird box

*Stardust Haiku*

the coldness
of a prayer stone . . .
steady drizzle

*Wales Haiku Journal*

spring epiphany
hidden in shadow
how tiny the toad

*Akitsu Quarterly*

the white lotus
weightless in dark water . . .
meditations

*Stardust Haiku*

setting a turtle
in better shadows
behind the clinic

*Modern Haiku*



the heavens . . .
a wild pony
. . . nodding

*Autumn Moon*



open gate
a yellow butterfly finds
the way

*Bottle Rockets*

# Bibliography

Baker, Brian. "Mount Pleasant Gargoyle a Graveyard Mystery." *Streeter*.
    January 8, 2017. https://streeter.ca/leaside/views/column/mount-
    pleasant-gargoyle-builds-a-mystery/.
Parrinder, Geoffrey ed.  *World Religions: From Ancient History to the Present*.
    New York: Newnes Books, 1971.